Perfect Italian is the third and final installment in Petrosino's series on heritage, identity and belonging. Previous books in the collection, also published by Sarabande, include White Blood: A Lyric of Virginia *(2020) and* Bright *(2022).*

Praise for *White Blood*

"Kiki Petrosino has been perfecting a form of weaponized valentine, a love poem armed with play and appraisal, ever since her amazing debut. Her poems charm and fillet. In *White Blood: A Lyric of Virginia* home is filled with history and possibility, 'that twoness one ever feels' in place and body. Both singular lyric poem and mercurial sequence featuring epistles, erasures, and sonnets, this book is wonderfully irreducible. It's further evidence of Kiki Petrosino's limitless, inimitable talent." —Terrance Hayes, author of *American Sonnets for My Past*

"Fueled by what it means to identify your own blood, *White Blood* is a masterful book of poems that excavates, resurrects, and stares clear-eyed into history. Petrosino's intricate attention to sound and the muscularity of the poetic line make these poems explode in both the ear and the heart. Here is a poet at her best." —Ada Limón, author of *The Carrying*

"This is an important and remarkable exploration of heritage."
—*Publishers Weekly*, starred review

"Petrosino composes poems that burn and sizzle, that pierce the reader with their masterful crafting and heightened vulnerability"
—*Poets & Writers*, "Between Worlds: A Q&A with Poet Kiki Petrosino"

Praise for *Bright*

"Kiki Petrosino's *Bright* is an astonishing lyric archive of the body—who it's made of; what's imposed upon it; what's extracted from it—the result of which is one of the most moving, and incisive documents on the brutalizing fictions of race that I've ever read. As formally experimental as survival is, *Bright* lights the ways our different bodies in different places at different times are forced again and again to negotiate and endure and evade and refuse those stories. Refusal the result of which is sometimes as beautiful, as luminous, as the book in your hands."
—Ross Gay, author of *The Book of Delights* and *Catalog of Unabashed Gratitude*

"Let me describe the powers of *Bright: A Memoir.* Within it, I find pages of strength (holding up a sentence of nearly unbearable weight, but not letting go), of restraint (knowing that the sentence must be held up alone), and of patience (all the measured breaths taken in order to reach that utterance). This book astonishes me. Kiki Petrosino is not only a superb writer, but a dazzling reader, and to glimpse, within this memoir, her way of perceiving what she encounters is revelatory. Whether parsing the details of a landscape or the notebooks of Thomas Jefferson, Petrosino finds within them more than what their authors meant to say. What she has to say—of childhood, history, race, family, literature, inheritance—is so immense you might be surprised it can be contained within a book of this size, but this is another of its powers. Open it up, and you'll find the expertly-compressed energy of its language expanding into a beautiful new shape, one you'll treasure." —Heather Christle, author of *The Crying Book*

"Award-winning poet Petrosino probes her identity as a poet and biracial woman in a slender, expressive memoir that swirls around the meaning of bright. . . . A spare, affecting, lyrical memoir." —*Kirkus Reviews*

"[A] stunning exploration. . . . [Petrosino's] work packs a hefty punch, offering a luminous descent into the complicated racial history of the United States and a nuanced path to a more expansive future. This challenging and soulful work shines with intellect." —*Publishers Weekly*, starred review

PERFECT ITALIAN

PERFECT ITALIAN

POEMS

KIKI PETROSINO

SARABANDE BOOKS *Louisville KY*

FIRST EDITION

Publisher's Cataloging-in-Publication Data
(Provided by Cassidy Cataloguing Services, Inc.)

Names: Petrosino, Kiki, 1979- author.
Title: Perfect Italian : poems / Kiki Petrosino.
Description: First edition. | Louisville, KY : Sarabande Books, [2026]
Identifiers: ISBN: 9781956046458 (paperback) | 9781956046465 (ebook)
Subjects: LCSH: Belonging (Social psychology) | Heredity. | Language and languages. | Citizenship. | Multiracial people. | Families. | Grief. | LCGFT: Poetry.
Classification: LCC: PS3616.E868 P47 2026 | DDC: 811/.6--dc23

Cover design by Emily Mahon.
Interior design by Erin Dorney.
Printed in the USA on acid-free paper.
Sarabande Books is a nonprofit literary organization.

The Kentucky Arts Council, the state arts agency, supports Sarabande Books with state tax dollars and federal funding from the National Endowment for the Arts.

KENTUCKY Arts COUNCIL

In Memoriam

Vincent Petrosino
1947–2025

my father

Oratorio

De Jure Sanguinis

To Think of Italy While Climbing the Saunders-Monticello Trail

Jus Soli

For the Reader

These poems ask questions about belonging. In this way, they are also concerned with family, and the law.

De jure sanguinis, Latin for "by right of blood," refers to a legal principle allowing a person's citizenship to derive from ancestry.

Conversely, jus soli ("by right of the soil") determines a person's citizenship according to their place of birth.

I was born in the United States of America, a jus soli country, as the descendant of free and enslaved Black Americans. I'm also the granddaughter and great-granddaughter of Italian ancestors. They came from Padula, a hillside town in the Vallo di Diano.

Like a poem, the law draws its columns and spheres. But nothing stays still. The human spirit, longing to tell its own story, breaks free from every constraint.

Syllable by syllable, love is the line I follow.

Perfect Italian

Poems

Libertà va cercando, ch'è sì cara .

Dante Alighieri, *Purgatorio* I.71

Oratorio

I came in at the end. No one around.
                    No one gone. Born already paddling. Where?

Out there to out there. Diasporic psalm
                    slipped from palm to palm. I wanted to write

a beautiful book. My letterforms blazed
                    & curved. And on the lake of my tongue, what

swans, expensive & pale, brooded over
                    my small clutch of speech. Some wishes translate

themselves from the air, yet will not be touched.
                    Mothers, Fathers: I have been so lonely.

De Jure Sanguinis

Heritage

I slide my mother tongue to the other
        side, crossing the Atlantic exactly
backwards. *Piano piano* I work my way
        under wax seals & ancestral damasks.
Slowly I seep, a stain, taking the shape
        of a long-lost lexical gloss. Remade
in my "colored" mouth, conjugated in
        wine, my vocab pours back into my glass.
Time reverses. The Old World breaks open.
        With my scallop shell, I scoop out the blood.

Mi Presento

I wasn't born with language, only blood.
          The way I always want to leave, like slow
honey. In spring, pink wounds appear inside
          a dogwood blossom just as it opens
its small handful of thunder. I peel back
          memory in cloudy shreds, trying to touch
the thick, clear fluid beneath: womb-water
          suspending light, attenuating sound
or so I hope. What I want to say dips
          so far into the page. I can't say where.

Heritage (Baltimore)

Sometimes the weather turned, & burned sugar
          floated on the air. Sometimes men knelt down
to weep alongside the water. Christ walked
          every night, past the old slaughterhouses
leaving footprints in the bloody sawdust
          which spilled from trucks & along passages
lined with brick. From inside out, in iron air
          language grew sideways, scarred & glittering
belly down, pulling its chain of wonders
          link by link from the depths of the city.

Literacy Narrative

The little bit I knew of Italy
        could fit on a triangle of white dough
once. I folded my floppy slice in half
        & bit down, Brooklyn-style. Blistered hard
into the crust, tiny cubes of spiced meat
        resolved into glyphs. I began to read
by edges & by crumbs. I picked out verbs
        & laid them along the rim of my plate.
No one helped. But no one really stopped me.
        Bit by bit, I scraped my way toward speech.

Garden of Inventions

Can you imagine? Da Vinci's Cradle—
        I gripped my safety bar, peered out, across
this theme park Italy (green shrubs, white plinths)
        a living jewel box, lit, for one stunned breath.
Weightless, circling, I lifted from myself
        in a clear arc, gathering height & distance
woodsmoke dissolving on the summer air
        music thinning to a gleam. How I looked
through a moment, to glimpse the rainswept path
        I would cross, petals falling all around.

Heritage (Brooklyn)

I'm trying to write about this constant
    howling I remember, just outside the
windows of my grandparents' apartment
    a sound, spanning the grid of gray-white sky
between high-rises, this vast whispering
    a soft ripping, as of cloth, or damp leaves
dark wheeze of somebody old & ailing
    in another room, another decade
this sorrow, seeping beneath the doorframe
    invisible, accusing, so *lonely*—

Beginner

I trace a silk thread back to language lab.
        I listen to dialogue, then soft cubes
of static. From these, I sculpt my replies
        & stick them to the backs of each cassette.
How it's done is how it's always been done.
        I do it. Portioned, polite. Agreeing
my nouns & verbs, drawing my first trembling
        loops of meaning. If I show up to this
like a houseguest, it'll be easy to
        take me & cut me out in little stars.

Chiave

My *nonna* & her pan full of breadcrumbs.
        Nonna of faith & Nonna among stars.
Nonna in her traveling dress, gold rosettes
        lifting off the fabric, blooming in air.
Tiny gold petals, gold bees thickening
        in purposeful dabs, gold light all around
clouding the kitchen & breading the fish
        gold pixels spilling down the countertop
gold notelets, gold capitals trembling
        into sounds I know & can—*almost*—touch.

Confession

When I get my conjugations just right
        my relief is the tail of a cooked shrimp
detaching from its shell: that hard, clockwise
        twist, the rest of the sentence following
delicate & opaque, curling inward
        as it cools. The good part of myself lives
here. In piles of ecstatic scraps. In speech
        that splits & peels. I test my fluency
by the kilo, sliding my knife between
        meat & carapace, never getting full.

Study Abroad

The night before I leave for Italy
    I lie in the dark, in the same body
I've always carried. I open my mouth
    & draw out the black petals of silence
which have bloomed around my grief. Dante cried
    for Virgil three times as the divine stars
swayed behind a veil of flowers. Some nights
    it's hard to hold the vanished forms I loved.
Lilies of water & lilies of breath
    hang in the air. No language touches them.

Descent

On the plane, I bring my hands to my lips
as the living green rushes all around
pressing every window. Still, still English
hovers behind my soft palate, bright gulps
of bewildered grammar from another
lifetime. Balancing meters from the earth
a stripe of sunrise lengthens down my neck.
I accept this first mark, first character
on my daylight page, runway blooming up
to catch me, my whole life touching down.

What Happens

Arriving in-country, among the steel
            combs of Mediterranean cypress
their distant spines raking the bright air

            (sudden taste in the mouth: pepper, wild game)

we wonder how much of this we can keep

            (tobacco, dried cherries, crumbled barley)

but nothing stays still. Not that trembling light
            scorching those sharp, Tuscan crowns of foliage
nor our own attention, splintered & stung—

            (black fruits black fruits black fruits black fruits black fruits)

Acclimation

I don't start to feel OK until bread
        & tomatoes, until the square bottle
of olive oil, until I can lean back
        to view the gold line of light two-thirds up
the spine of each palazzo. Above us
        umbrella pines are having their own day
roving & tangling, soft in the clear air.
        How am I supposed to get over this?
From my spot on the street, I find the edge
        of ecstatic silence & pull it through.

Straniera

At Roma Termini, nobody cares
        that I'm a "heritage learner." Pigeons
swoop as I stammer in my green sandals.
        I have lost the ultimate train. I'd like
just one grandma to scoop me up, to call
        in her trilling notes, to clasp my strange hand
in hers. Grammar of luck, gold coin inside
        la coincidenza—I feel it all
with my wild nerves. *Tomorrow, madam.*
        Who speaks of loneliness? Rattle, drawl, coo.

Cultural Study

In this country, I slip around small talk
        lowering a flower mask over my
New World accent. The best compliment is
        when no one notices if I'm alive
or just a quiet smudge. I overhear
        some new synonyms for watermelon—
anguria, melone di pane—
        languid syllables, rich & sweetening.
By the kitchen wall, in a shady spot
        I cut into thick, gold slices of sound.

New World

Now that I'm here, I carry no real weight.
            The chocolate bars are smaller & less sweet.
It doesn't take me long to whittle down
            to the pretty bones: clavicle & throat
glowing fashionably. In my tank top
            I walk everywhere & surprise myself
when I only want some plain strawberries.
            In the morning, by the fountain, I cry
less. With a book of sonnets in my hands
            I proceed down light & dark passages.

Sottopassaggio

The color of the year in this country
          is a green I follow from street to street
& underground, to the tiled vestibule
          of the metro. The name of an icy
salad lingers on my tongue, an ornate
          heaviness. I want to buy this strange green
blossoming from the necks of people's coats
          (is it the same silk shirt on everyone?)
& start to try to ask. Across the blank
          windows of passing trains, my face repeats.

De Jure Sanguinis

I wonder if the other side knows me
        or wants to know. The air never quivers
with a color I've worn. My birth? A mischief
        at the tail end of a troublesome chain.
Hey. Do you know what a chain means to me?
        Observe my hands, veined with a gold you can't
deny. It means we can't keep talking past
        each other. Except we do. All day long
we weave our marvelous opacity.
        I can't feel your palm through this window glass.

Sirocco

Alone, I follow flat walls. Touch plaster
    as green doors of silence open inward.
I don't know what I mean to anyone
    & that draws me down little alleyways.
Time slows & darkens, like red waves of dust
    brushed up the flanks of a wayside chapel.
Whoever wrote my audio guide knew
    these streets, the *staccato* of bikes & cabs
but not how tired I would get from trying
    to keep cheerful inside my loneliness.

Campanilismo

There is a moment, early on, when all
          language dissolves. I climb up the main road
striking my heels against black cobblestones
          until I reach the church, hung with ribbons
from a First Communion
                              —when?—
                                        this morning.
I hurry toward the sanctuary
          my breath catching in little, snagging loops
flower garlands tumbling in the hot breeze
          with no bell-song, no voices following
my small heartbeat, my procession of one.

Expatriate

Passing all the closed storefronts *in centro*
        steel gratings rolled down the dim ledge of dawn
I think of never coming back here
        not to the botanical garden with its
cement beds, nor to the ridged metal seats
        of the café, where I try to erase
this warble from my voice. The kind of day
        I have depends on who's nice to me
& the city's mood shifts in its rain-mesh.
        No one who loves me is here to hear this.

Solo Travel

In Venice, I buy a leather journal
        its pebbled grain already soft, its red
ecclesiastical & insistent
        upon formalities I'm unprepared
to ratify with my American
        essence, though my own hide be no less real
no less aglow, no less intertextual.
        I read myself by lagoon light, spitball
as to my destiny, which grows less clear
        the longer I stand here without speaking.

Selva Erronea

Just when I start to think about staying
  the dark spikes of green cypress rise up.
At every crossing, they split the dim sky
  into clauses, interrupting my prayer
with their narrow teeth. Why did I come here
  to this austere edge? Some glint in the trees
must want to keep me out of my right mind.
  When I think of my mother missing me
& how I choose to keep on staying gone—
  Some days, I don't put down a single word.

To Think of Italy While Climbing the Saunders-Monticello Trail

*

two Piedmonts nearly
          touch across green water

I watch my hands fill up
          with wilderness

*

these mountains have given us
          so much & we

will not even give ourselves
          to each other

*

what I have to say belongs
          to these mountains

remember how it happened
          a mixed marriage

*

marl of sand & silence
          limestone, longing

I turn my face
          dissolve into the Blue Ridge

*

in the passage that opens
 when I pronounce

Africa, America
 worlds within worlds *Italia*

*

triple the stitch
 tethering me to this spot

slick of beeswax
 conditioning my life-thread

*

in the first Piedmont, a man
          was poor if he

owned just one side of the same
          ancestral slope

*

what of the other Piedmont
          new, dipped in green

land where families bought &
          sold each other

*

Jefferson filled his coat
        with Piedmontese rice

dreamed of fortunes sifting through
        rough teeth, iron combs

*

In Albemarle
        buttered grains heaped on white plates

Dante: *as sun*
        unseals an imprint in snow

*

five green gallons
    of olive oil yearly

so “necessary of life”
    Jefferson ate

*

Italian friends
    sent seeds from their warm country

who tended those
    fruits unfolding into light

*

it's true I fell
in love with all that red earth

as I watched my
tears soften into the bricks

*

or: I was there
when they scooped me from the ground

fingerprints along each edge
dotting my name

*

worlds within worlds
    worlds within worlds, so near

but not quite touching, moving
    in close orbits

*

turning buffet
    slave ship turning downriver

turn my wonder
    & my sorrow & my dread

*

cessa crudel
his map of blue Africa

lost, pointed face
cinched coastline, hills of soft air

*

anything you want could fit
inside that shape

desire, destiny, desire
cessa crudel

*

let me tell you
        what's growing in the archive

fascination
        furrows of ink, name on name

*

here's history
        its perpetual machine

slicing the past into stars
        of amethyst

*

surging landscape
        at the edge of my hearing

lexical blue
        rising from plantation ground

*

the "South Piazza"
        arcaded *loggia* of glass

the plain workbench
        where Jefferson made keys, locks

*

Italian seeds
    embedded in commonwealth

I open the garden door
    to study this

*

my feet fit inside phonemes
    my face: sunburned

al cor gentil
    I repair, following shades

*

some histories are sonic
    I can trace them

in two languages I hold
    the great poets

*

who composed these
    windows cut out against sky

light playing on
    passages of textured glass

*

"Cherries of different kinds from
　　　　Italy," cracked

from their small pits
　　　　& some planted as whole stones

*

In Brooklyn, Nonno forged locks
　　　　& iron screens

which let the sunlight drift down
　　　　in clear petals

*

when did my family become
white, become mist

their folded names
walled orchards, what did they want

*

look: the high, frilled
stalks of *cavolo nero*

seem to cluster
around formal mysteries

*

always, always
    between courses of old brick

distant syntax
    presses memory from the hours

*

knife-pleats of rain
    cannot divide self from self

the mountains bend
    into a haze of witness

*

now, as bee-songs
knot the air, I count up all

my faults, flowers crisping like
bursts of speech

*

last night the rosemary wept
in little spikes

green wish, white wish
to be home in my being

*

it's lonely when
 the last visitors depart

& the poplars
 close around their own beauty

*

at my ear's cusp
 in this orthogonal space

Italian words
 alight from my inquiry

*

memory crosses seams of air
        no—marbles in

a seed fastens
        greening the burial ground

*

the ancestor
        pulls a fig straight off its branch

why not she says
        biting through *isn't it mine*

Jus Soli

Aural Domain

Blood isn't everything. Blood is under
        everything. The bells of Nonno's city
ring in rivulets, each toll a message:
        Come to church. Prayer is better than sleeping.
For a whole century, the streets emptied.
        Even Nonno climbed down to the ocean.
Still, the tongues of bells move in their quadrants
        cutting the same arc through shadowy air
circling the thin red poppies in the grass.
        No matter where I am, I'm always here.

Midlife

I'm telling my friend about this life stage
          how sometimes I sense new luck on the air
like the watery scent of melting snow.
          I tell her: *We have a chance to do things*
different this time, because we know much more
          about love. Like, we really, really know
how to love now & my friend, beautiful
          in the cold, oblique light of early spring
turns to me & says *Yeah, but I don't want*
          to live through any of this shit again.

Heritage (Louisa)

It wasn't until I was an adult
        that I heard my first doxology. Christ
streamed through stained glass, painting my hymnal with
        gold passages. Still, I couldn't follow
the order of worship, so I just watched
        color pooling on *creatures here below*
as if the light were leading my lesson
        threading all the way back to that first place
first opening in the trees, first arbor
        impossible to touch, yet close as skin.

Atmospheric Perspective

I'm listening to my friend explain how
just because someone has died, it doesn't
mean the end, how you go on, you go on
trying to reach them. Da Vinci believed
all edges fade to softness. He rendered
distant objects in lighter tones, adored
the vapor he saw sifting among forms.
I, too, wish to touch that dissolving haze
where language breaks into blue particles
& returns as pure witness, scattered light.

First Morning in Nonno's Town

So absent, his absence takes many shapes:
          gold stroke of sunlight on a wooden chair
thumbprint of silence pressed into the grass.
          At breakfast, a green pear, freckled, heavy
presents itself, but refuses to slice.
          I walk to the meadow's edge, my cargo
jacket studded with burrs & weedy thorns
          verbs collecting at the back of my throat.
There's nowhere to sit & no one to see.
          My shadow thins toward a focused point.

Atmospheric Perspective (II)

Tonight, I folded Nonno's death record
		into a fireproof sleeve, the words *hanged self*
turned inward, close. Now it's quiet again.
		The letterforms climb down, into the dark
between pages. Some weep. Some silently
		adore their own capitals, architraves.
Still others move in oblique arcs of thought
		turning & tracing some bright, eternal
dialect of air. They pass beyond speech
		just as I mark out my first syllables.

Midlife (II)

Because I wanted to forget my home
            I swapped my colonial tongue for this
other one. Threaded myself through keyholes
            into gardens reserved for private use
& learned to read the play of light on tombs.
            Now, when I think of that time, I'm the wren
nesting in the notch of a great serif
            my feathers blurred, my crinkle of bright song
unfolding from the inside out, a *churr*
            too deep for anyone but God to hear.

Exchange

English is a fine language, they tell me
    per fare il commercio. I count coins
gently & in error, rolling them from
    palm to palm until they clink to the floor.
Wish I could squint, like a mercantile wife
    in a salty township, bargaining hard
for her beer & her ropes of tobacco
    but I'm a soft one, slow in the mornings
chastened by the coldness of winter light
    on granite. Nothing here is my business.

Serata

In Nonno's town, I buy a book on roots.
        I buy a book on fruits. I buy lip balm
made from regional lavender & booze
        recreated from monastic receipts.
Here, my tears fall in unpredictable
        waveforms, my thoughts grow woody, botanic.
As the main piazza fills up at night
        folks talk, their words candied with Silentium.
One father says: *Go, travel the whole world*
        then, at sixty, you'll come back here to live.

At Autogrill

I'm learning to keep my loneliness
            to myself. Black dawn splits into slices
of neon black. I try to smile, holding
            my tongue fast behind my teeth. Why can't I
just enjoy the long, sweet strands of chestnut
            paste, curled up like sleeping animals
in glass cups, the cold thimblefuls of plain
            water to rinse the palate? In beauty
my sadness accretes, making soft hillocks
            of English I climb, & then climb again.

Scamels

You won't feel like this forever, unless
        forever is here. Follow the dark blue
blades of kale, the flat dials of sunflowers
        leading back to speech, or its underside.
Love translated you across an ocean
        & now you cannot really come away
or say how, exactly, your love began.
        Was it music in the mouth, or weeping
in the blood? The ancestral body splits
        into water & seeds, pure syllables.

The Site of Memory

If I hold still, I can almost touch it.
          Hovering at the blue edge of daylight:
a glint, or a curve, the exact texture
          of my thoughts. Cool on the air, & brighter
than the silver slants of seabirds (far off
          filling the sky over the bay with script)
brighter, even, than the water itself.
          Green-gray, glass-gray, this thing I know, nearly
but cannot name. It slips past me just when
          I feel its gaze—that weight—& turn to look—

Recitativo Secco

I fold back my wings. I try to translate.
          What tremor in Nonno's palm. What wing-flick
whitening the silence between heartbeats.
          In Nonno's town, I feel the house martins
arriving on daylight air. They scoop up
          mud for their nests, neat convex cups stuck hard
to the sides of inhabited homes. Now
          when I press my ear to the past, a scrape
of sound emerges from the layered dark.
          It is mine to say what a bloodline is.

Continuo

Two languages hang in a grassy field.
Which will be taken & which will be left?

Two languages with skin like blue churches.
Which will be taken & which will be left?

Two languages braiding into themselves.
Which will be taken & which will be left?

Two languages spinning on belts of reeds.
Which will be taken & which will be left?

Two languages seceding from the neck.
Which will be taken & which will be left?

Nocturne

In the night garden, the word for *bud* sounds
just like the word for *gem*. I wake, thinking
of the florin. I've studied diligence
by driving one rare amaro after
another down my throat. Woody, blackened
visions came to me in the thorn forest
where my grief curled into a twisted hum.
An argument about the past breaks out
tonight, hounds racing over patterned mulch.
I rise into the air & never rest.

Atmospheric Perspective (III)

Once, I asked Nonno about black roses—
          do they exist? *Sure, on the other side.*
But when I traveled there, I couldn't see
          all he meant. Back then, I sounded out each
word before speaking, weighed my appetite
          in *etti*, pretended to like the tripes
draped over my plate. Now, I'm saying black
          roses exist. I've felt them break open
in sentences, along the borders of
          vision. I've heard them speak inside my name.

Elegy

for my father

Now that I've told you all about my heart
    I await your next question. But when
you start to speak, a coastline appears.
    I travel it, electrical, no shoes
skimming the beach & the forested slopes
    laid out exactly like the mountain towns
the young have fled. And where have you gone to?
    When I arrive at this new silence, it's
so much smaller without you, scraped clean.
    My heart blurs, wishing to be there & here.

Heritage (Padula)

The paperbacks here are so delicate
I'm afraid to open them. I climb down
each page, like the many staircases
of Nonno's town, careful of my ankles
as stony treads dissolve to white gravel
then grass, which I cross, touching passages
of music tumbled with unfamiliar
earth. I still pray for Nonno in English
whenever I read woodsmoke on the air.
I say his name & a little light comes.

Primavera

In Virginia, the cherry trees put on
        their huge pink prom dresses for just a few
slow nights each spring. I pull up my folding
        chair, lean into rosy shadows, edges
of starlight catching the outer petals.
        I want the blossoms to have some fragrance
& I almost sense it: a shred, a haze
        overruled by the green sobs of cut grass.
I want to believe I'm doing some good.
        My sandals leave diagrams in the weeds.

Aria

In the window-light: green bird to green wire.
I watch as my page goes bright with stillness.

Mineral wing, glass wing. I am writing:
Some of us carry the last hazelnuts

in our mouths, intending to bury them
between the city & the mountainside.

My grandmother wished to become a bird.
Can I go where wishes go? My feathers

gather & settle, gather & settle
all around the aleph of my longing.

Notes

De Jure Sanguinis

"I came in at the end": This line comes from the first episode of the HBO drama series *The Sopranos,* created by David Chase. Season 1, episode 1, "Pilot," aired in the United States on January 10, 1999.

"the other / side": My grandfather, Prospero Petrosino, was born in Padula, Italy, in 1908. In conversation, he often referred to Italy as "the other side."

"my scallop shell": The white scallop shell is a pilgrimage symbol. In the Middle Ages, pilgrims en route to Santiago de Compostela, Spain, used empty shells as vessels for eating or begging. In Italy, pilgrims making an intermediate sojourn to Pistoia to visit the tomb of Saint James the Greater attached scallop shells to their cloaks as proof of their journey along the Cammino di San Jacopo.

"burned sugar / floated on the air": Baltimore's Domino Sugar refinery, located at 1100 Key Highway along the city's Inner Harbor waterfront, was established in 1922. The factory refines nearly one million pounds of raw sugar per year.

"the old slaughterhouses": Historically, slaughterhouses and meatpacking facilities were located in several Baltimore neighborhoods. One of the oldest and largest operations, the Esskay plant at 3800 East Baltimore Street, was active throughout the twentieth century.

"Garden of Inventions / Da Vinci's Cradle": Busch Gardens, near Williamsburg, Virginia, is a 422-acre theme park developed by Anheuser-Busch and owned by United Parks and Resorts. The now-defunct Garden of Inventions was a section of the park's Italian "village," and featured rides inspired by Leonardo da Vinci's sketchbooks. The Da Vinci's Cradle ride was active at Busch Gardens from 1983 to 2022.

"take me & cut me out in little stars": The line is adapted from William

Shakespeare's *The Tragedy of Romeo and Juliet,* 3.2.24. I referred to the Folger Shakespeare Library's edition of the play, edited by Barbara A. Mowat and Paul Werstine in 2014.

"Dante cried / for Virgil three times": Here I offer my interpretation of the passage in Dante Alighieri's *Purgatorio* XXX, 49–51.

"the air never quivers / with a color I've worn": The image is adapted from a line in Isak Dinesen's *Out of Africa* (Putnam, 1937).

"Selva Erronea": The title comes from Dante's *Convivio* IV, xxiv, 12, as found on The Princeton Dante Project website.

To Think of Italy While Climbing the Saunders-Monticello Trail

The prevalence of eleven-syllable patterns in this part of the book is inspired by the *stornello,* an Italian folk form which gained popularity in the nineteenth century in that country. I call my poem a "stornello sbagliato," as I've stretched the "rules" of the original in realizing this New World interpretation.

The Saunders-Monticello trailhead is located at 503 Thomas Jefferson Parkway in Charlottesville, Virginia.

"two Piedmonts": The term refers to a geographical region at the foot of a mountain range. Northwest Italy (at the foot of the Alps) and Central Virginia (between the Coastal Plain and the Blue Ridge Mountains) are each called "Piedmont."

"Jefferson filled his coat / with Piedmontese rice": In 1787, while serving as America's Minister to France, Thomas Jefferson toured northwest Italy. He was interested in sourcing a prized rice varietal there, but in his July 14 letter to Edward Rutledge, Jefferson reports that because of prohibitions on the export of unmilled grains, "I could only bring off as much as my coat and surtout pockets would hold." The full text of the letter is available on the National Archives Founders Online website.

"as sun / unseals an imprint in snow": The reference comes from Dante's *Paradiso,* XXXIII, 64. To craft my line, I referred to the 2007 Anchor Books translation by Robert Hollander and Jean Hollander.

"five green gallons / of olive oil yearly": Jefferson regularly imported from Europe specialty grocery items for Monticello's kitchens. For years, he corresponded with Stephen Cathalan, an American consul in Marseilles. His letters often included orders for Smyrna raisins, Italian cheese and pasta, and French olive oil. In one such letter, dated May 26, 1819, Jefferson requests "5. gallons of oil of Aix." The full text of the letter is available on the National Archives Founders Online website.

"necessary of life": The quoted phrase comes from Jefferson's letter to Thomas Jefferson Randolph, dated April 16, 1810. The full text of the letter is available on the National Archives Founders Online website.

"turning buffet": This term refers to the revolving door, fitted with shelving, located in Monticello's dining room. According to the Thomas Jefferson Foundation's Monticello.org, "It allowed enslaved domestic servants to remove empty serving dishes from the first course and to place foods for the second course on the shelves and then rotate the door into the dining room." For more information, see the "Revolving Serving Door" entry within Monticello.org's "Thomas Jefferson Encyclopedia."

"*cessa crudel*": The phrase, which means "cease, cruel one," comes from the eighteenth-century Italian art song "Caro Mio Ben," attributed to Giuseppe or Tommaso Giordani. In the track "Daughter," on the album *Cowboy Carter,* Beyoncé Giselle Knowles-Carter interprets an excerpt from this song. *Cowboy Carter* was released March 29, 2024, by Parkwood Entertainment and Columbia Records.

"his map of blue Africa": Jefferson displayed his 1802 map of Africa, drawn by London mapmaker Aaron Arrowsmith, in Monticello's Entrance Hall. For more information about the map collection, see the entry on "Aaron Arrowsmith Maps of Africa, Asia, and Europe" within Monticello.org's "Thomas Jefferson Encyclopedia."

"amethyst": In Query VI of *Notes on the State of Virginia* (1785), Jefferson counts amethysts as a "frequent" example of the commonwealth's "subterranean riches."

"South Piazza": This was Jefferson's name for what Monticello.org describes as the "small, glass-enclosed arched loggia" where Jefferson, in retirement, situated his greenhouse and personal workbench. For more information, see the entry on "Greenhouses" within Monticello.org's "Thomas Jefferson Encyclopedia."

"where Jefferson made keys, locks": Isaac Granger, Jefferson's former enslaved blacksmith, noted in his memoir that "My Old Master was neat a hand as ever you see to make keys and locks and small chains, iron and brass." I referred to the HathiTrust Digital Library's version of *Memoirs of a Monticello Slave: As Dictated to Charles Campbell in the 1840s by Isaac, One of Thomas Jefferson's Slaves* (Rayford W. Logan, ed., University of Virginia Press, 1951).

"*al cor gentil* / I repair": The reference is to Guido Guinizelli's canzone, "Al cor gentil rempaira sempre amore," collected in *Rime* (Edoardo Sanguineti, ed., Einaudi, 1986).

"cherries of different kinds from / Italy": The line comes from a March 31, 1774, entry in Jefferson's horticultural journal. I referred to *The Garden and Farm Books of Thomas Jefferson* (Robert C. Baron, ed., Fulcrum, 1987).

Jus Soli

"Aural Domain": The phrase comes from Mary Ruefle's essay "Hell's Bells: Notes on Tone," which appeared in the Spring 2019 issue of *Sewanee Review*.

"creatures here below": This line comes from a hymn written by Anglican bishop Thomas Ken. It was first published as "Morning Hymn" in *A*

Manual of Prayers for the Use of the Scholars of Winchester College (1674). Now known as the doxology, the hymn is sung as part of the worship service of many Christian denominations. I heard it sung at Wayland Baptist Church in Louisa, Virginia.

"Silentium": This refers to the herbal liqueur developed by the 1306 Project in Padula, Italy. Inspired by the legacy of Padula's Certosa di San Lorenzo, a historic Carthusian monastery and UNESCO World Heritage Site, the Silentium "elixir" incorporates botanicals sourced from the Southern Apennines.

"Scamels": This word comes from William Shakespeare's *The Tempest,* 2.1.178. I referred to The Folger Shakespeare Library's edition of the play, edited by Barbara A. Mowat and Paul Werstine in 2004.

"The Site of Memory": The title is from Toni Morrison's 1987 lecture, published in *Inventing the Truth: The Art and Craft of Memoir* (William Zinsser, ed., Houghton Mifflin, 1998.

"Which will be taken & which will be left?": The line is adapted from Matthew 24:40.

Acknowledgments

I would like to thank the editors of the journals where earlier versions of these poems were published:

"First Morning in Nonno's Town" appeared in Issue 98 of *The Louisville Review*, guest edited by Jeffrey Skinner.

"Heritage," "Cultural Study," and "New World" appeared in the Circuit 5 issue of *Solid State*, edited by Matt Hart.

"Scamels" appeared online as "from 'De Jure Sanguinis'" on July 23, 2025, in *Poem-a-Day*, a feature of the Academy of American Poets' website, guest curated by Khadijah Queen.

"Mi Presento," "Study Abroad," and "Selva Erronea" appeared online in the Summer 2025 issue of *Under a Warm Green Linden*, edited by Christopher Nelson.

The first two sections of "To Think of Italy While Climbing the Saunders-Monticello Trail" were published as a single poem in the anthology *You Are Here: Poetry in the Natural World*, edited by the twenty-fourth United States Poet Laureate, Ada Limón, and published by Milkweed Editions and the Library of Congress in 2024.

Portions of "To Think of Italy While Climbing the Saunders-Monticello Trail" were published as an essay, "The Red Earth of Terra," and as poems, "Terra (3)," "Terra (4)," and "Terra (5)," in the Winter 2023 issue of *Italian Americana: Cultural and Historical Review*, published by the University of Illinois Press.

Many thanks to the University of Virginia's College of Arts & Sciences, the UVA Department of English, and the Virginia Commission for the Arts for their support of my research and writing.

I'm grateful for travel opportunities provided by the University of Iowa's International Writing Program, Art Center Padula, and The American

School in Switzerland.

My friends and family have offered me endless love and hospitality throughout my writing process. Thank you to my husband, Philip Miller; to my mother, Patricia Petrosino; to my sister, Francesca Gamber, & family; to the Palumbos of Brooklyn; and to Nino Melito Petrosino & family of Padula.

Because you are, I am.

KIKI PETROSINO is the author of several poetry collections which include *Perfect Italian* (2026) *White Blood: A Lyric of Virginia* (2020), *Witch Wife* (2017), *Hymn for the Black Terrific* (2013), and *Fort Red Border (2009)*, and the memoir *Bright* (2022) all published by Sarabande Books. She holds graduate degrees from the University of Chicago and the University of Iowa Writer's Workshop. She is a Professor of Poetry at the University of Virginia where she teaches in the MFA and undergraduate Creative Writing programs. Petrosino is the recipient of a DeWitt Wallace/Readers Digest fellowship from MacDowell artist residency, a Pushcart Prize, a Fellowship in Creative Writing from the National Endowment for the Arts, the UNT Rilke Prize, & the Spalding Prize, among other honors.

Sarabande Books is an award-winning, nonprofit independent literary press founded in 1994 in Louisville, Kentucky. With nearly three hundred titles in print, we have earned a dedicated readership and a national reputation as a publisher of diverse forms and innovative voices, creating lasting editions that honor exceptional writing. Through our free arts programming, we are proud to invest in emerging writers, and serve as an educational resource locally and nationally.

www.ingramcontent.com/pod-product-compliance
Lightning Source LLC
Chambersburg PA
CBHW010743270426
43918CB00019B/268
* 2 3 7 0 0 0 2 1 9 5 1 0 2 *